# Hamilton Beach Breakfast

## Sandwich Maker Cookbook 2021

### 365 Days of Affordable, Quick and Healthy Recipes to Boost Your Energy & Live a Healthy Lifestyle

by
Jonalyn Schismenos

# TABLE OF CONTENTS

# INTRODUCTION

They say that breakfast is the most important meal of the day. Unfortunately for most people mornings are hectic, especially families with kids. So how do you cope with breakfast pangs of hunger? If you're like most people, you've got to rush through the meal, swallow in the kitchen anything handy, or grab a quick, on-the-go bite.

That is where Hamilton Beach's Breakfast Sandwich Maker comes to the rescue. It is all about making a sandwich for a fresh breakfast that you can grab and go. On the fixings, simply choose your bread and layer: egg, cheese, precooked meat or the ingredients of your choice. Your perfectly assembled breakfast sandwich is ready for meal in five minutes or less. Your breakfast sandwich can be customized with a virtually endless variety of fresh ingredients. Now you know why everyone who loves breakfast sandwiches desires this product in their kitchen!

Don't let another morning pass by without Hamilton Beach's Breakfast Sandwich Maker. It enables you, in the comfort of your kitchen, enjoy a homemade breakfast sandwich, made your way. Because all removable parts go into the dishwasher, cleanup is simple.

# BENEFITS OF THE HAMILTON BEACH BREAKFAST SANDWICH MAKER

## Two sandwiches are better than one

Nobody, especially children, likes to wait for the breakfast. Now you can simultaneously produce and serve two hot and toasty sandwiches. Each of the sandwiches can be tailored to individual tastes, so each person can have their favorite. Even if you don't have time to sit down and eat breakfast at home, you can have two sandwiches for taking to work or school in about five minutes. One to cook? A single sandwich can be prepared by Breakfast Sandwich Maker too.

## Control what's inside your breakfast sandwiches

Do you really know what those restaurants, drive-thru, and store-bought sandwiches are all about? Thanks to the Breakfast Sandwich Maker, wondering about questionable or mysterious ingredients is no longer an issue. This is because you can make a breakfast sandwich (or two) with your own fresh ingredients quickly and easily, starting now. Only preheat the Breakfast Sandwich Maker, add ingredients of your preference and breakfast is ready in five minutes or less.

## Go healthy or hearty, depending on your mood

The Breakfast Sandwich Maker will help if you want to try healthier alternatives to the breakfast and consume less processed food. Your sandwiches might include full grain English muffins or bagels, low-fat cheese, egg whites, and veggies, lean meat, or a vegetarian option. On the other side,

7

the Breakfast Sandwich Maker is happy to oblige if you want to indulge in a satisfying, protein-packed sandwich. Use a whole egg and layer on your favorite cheese and meat to make that type of breakfast sandwich. You can also use a pancake on your finished sandwich as bread, and add the syrup. What you make is entirely up to you, and how you eat it. Since you can produce two at once, you can customize each of them to your liking.

**Make breakfast sandwiches the easy way**

If you've ever prepared breakfast sandwiches at home, you know this is a multi-step process that often requires more than one bread pan and a bread toaster. And that means cleaning multiple pans, too. When you've got extra time and energy to spare in the morning, that's fine. Even when you don't, what about mornings? Thanks to the five-minute cooking time and easy cleanup, you can still whip up two delicious sandwiches for breakfast. Know exactly how long the built in timer can be set in half-minute increments until breakfast is ready. When your sandwiches are ready, one tone sounds.

**Unlimited combinations for any taste**

Combining fresh ingredients with versatility makes the Breakfast Sandwich Maker the perfect breakfast solution for people of all ages. Each sandwich can be personalized to the adult, kid, day of the week or mood. People who own one say they have fun experimenting with various foods and flavours to make unique combinations of sandwiches. But if you're not inclined to create your own sandwich breakfast recipe, then you're in luck. At www. HamiltonBeach.com, try one of the recipes in the Use & Care guide or go to the Breakfast Sandwich Maker Receive collection.

**Easy Cleanup**

Unplug unit and allow to cool when finished cooking. To remove any baked-on ingredients using a plastic or wooden utensil. Hold bottom handle to open, then lift straight up, to remove the ring assembly for cleaning in or by hand in the dishwasher. For easier cleanup, before use and after washing spray rings and cooking plate with nonstick spray.

# IMPORTANT TIPS & TRICKS OF THE HAMILTON BEACH BREAKFAST SANDWICH MAKER

*Tips for use*

Extra-large eggs or extremely cold ingredients may prolong the cooking time. Bread with higher fat content, fewer ingredients, scrambled eggs, egg whites and precooked ingredients can shorten cooking time. Do not use appliance unattended. When any appliance is used by or near children, close supervision is required. For air circulation, provide 4 to 6 inches of air space over, behind and on both sides during use. When not in use, unplug from outlet.

# CLASSIC BREAKFAST SANDWICHES

## Egg and Cheese Breakfast Sandwiches

Prep/Cook Time: 45 mins, Serves: 12 Sandwiches

### Ingredients

- English Muffins
- Large eggs
- Cheese (I used about 10 ounces for 12 sandwiches.)
- Butter, or olive oil (optional)

### Instructions

- Lightly oil a muffin tin and crack an egg in each tin.

- Bake the muffin tin with eggs in a 350 degree oven for 10-15 minutes. Depending on your egg size, start checking them early to make sure they are cooked through. Try not to overcook them!

- Slice all the muffins and toast them in the oven for 10 minutes or you can toast them one at a time if you want.

- Add an egg, grated cheese, and any protein or veggies that you want to each sandwich.

- If you want to eat one right away, I recommend sticking it in the oven as a sandwich for 5-10 minutes to melt the cheese and everything.

- You can also stick all your sandwiches on a baking sheet and stick it in the freezer. Leave them in the freezer until they are frozen, about an hour. Then wrap each sandwich individually in plastic or foil and store all the individually wrapped sandwiches in a freezer safe bag.

- When reheating, you can microwave if you're in a hurry, but it'll make the muffin soggy. If you can plan ahead a bit, bake the sandwich at 350 degrees for about 25 minutes. You can even keep it wrapped in the foil if you used foil to store the sandwiches.

*Nutrition Info*

Calories: 322, Fat: 31g, Carbohydrates: 10g net, Protein: 16g

# Classic Breakfast Sandwich

Prep/Cook Time 18 minutes, Servings 4 sandwiches

## Ingredients

- o 2 teaspoons butter
- o 4 large eggs
- o salt & pepper to taste
- o 2 tablespoons water
- o 4 slices cheddar cheese
- o 4 slices Canadian bacon or 4 slices ham
- o 4 English muffins split

Sandwich Sauce

- o ⅓ cup mayonnaise
- o 1 tablespoon ketchup
- o dash of hot sauce

## Instructions

- • Mix sandwich sauce ingredients and set aside.

- Place muffins on a baking sheet, split side up and place under the broiler 2-3 minutes or until lightly crisped. Remove from the oven and spread each with sandwich sauce. Top 4 halves with Canadian bacon or ham and top 4 with cheese.
- Heat butter in a small non-stick skillet over medium heat.
- Crack eggs into the skillet and season with salt & pepper. Allow to cook about 1 minute to set the edges. Add 2 tablespoons water and cover with a lid. Cook 3-5 minutes or just until the yolks begin to set.
- While eggs are cooking, place English muffins back under the broiler to melt the cheese and heat the bacon.
- Add egg to each sandwich and serve!

*Nutrition Info*

Calories: 395, Carbohydrates: 28g, Protein: 16g, Fat: 24g, Saturated Fat: 6g, Cholesterol: 192mg, Sodium: 762mg, Calcium: 61mg, Iron: 1mg

# Fried Egg Sandwich

Prep/Cook Time: 15 mins, Servings: 4

## Ingredients

- o 2 teaspoons butter
- o 4 large eggs eggs
- o 4 slices processed American cheese
- o 8 slices toasted white bread
- o salt and pepper to taste
- o 2 tablespoons mayonnaise
- o 2 tablespoons ketchup

## Instructions

- In a large skillet, melt butter over medium high heat. Crack eggs in pan and cook to desired firmness. Just before eggs are cooked, place a slice of cheese over each egg.
- After cheese has melted, place each egg on a toasted slice of bread. Season eggs with salt and pepper. Spread mayonnaise and ketchup on remaining slices of bread and cover eggs with bread to make 4 sandwiches. Serve warm.

*Nutrition Info :* 385.6 calories; protein 16.6g 33% DV; carbohydrates 28.2g 9% DV; fat 23g 35% DV; cholesterol 220.6mg

# Healthy Caprese Breakfast Sandwich

Prep/Cook Time 20 minutes, Servings 6 servings

## Ingredients

- 6 Dave's Killer Bread Organic English Muffins
- fllaxseed oil or olive oil
- 2 avocados mashed
- 18 slices fresh mozzarella cheese
- 3 tomatoes sliced
- balsamic glaze
- kosher salt and freshly ground black pepper
- 6 eggs fried, hard boiled, scrambled, poached, or cooked to your liking
- 12 slices prosciutto
- 1/2 cup fresh basil leaves

## Instructions

- Toast the English muffins. For each English muffin sandwich, drizzle one half of the English muffin with flaxseed oil or olive oil. Spread 1-2 tablespoons of the mashed avocado on the other side of the muffin then layer with 2-3 slices of mozzarella, 3 slices of tomato, and drizzle with the balsamic glaze and sprinkle with kosher salt and pepper.

- Top with one egg and the prosciutto and sprinkle with fresh torn pieces of basil leaves. Top with the other English muffin half. Serve warm, chilled, or at room temperature.

*Recipe Notes*

You can make these sandwiches ahead and wrap tightly in plastic wrap and refrigerate for up to 3 days.

## *Nutrition Info*

Calories 373 Calories from Fat 198, Fat 22g, Saturated Fat 5g, Cholesterol 176mg, Sodium 402mg, Potassium 688mg, Carbohydrates 31g, Fiber 9g, Sugar 6g, Protein 15g

Prep/Cook Time: About 1 hr Active: 15 mins
Serves: 1 Sandwiches

## Ingredients

- o   1 teaspoon Sriracha hot sauce
- o   2 tablespoons Hellmann's mayonnaise
- o   1 1/2 tablespoons unsalted butter
- o   1 medium yellow onion, sliced thin
- o   3 farm-fresh eggs
- o   2 tablespoons thinly sliced chives
- o   Kosher salt
- o   1 brioche bun
- o   1 thick slice sharp cheddar cheese

## Instructions

To make the sauce:

- • Combine the Sriracha and mayonnaise in a small bowl. Whisk until the mixture is even in color. Set aside.

To caramelize the onion:

- • Set a sauté pan over medium-high heat. When the pan is hot add 1/2 tablespoon of the butter and let it melt. Add the onion and reduce the heat to low. Cook, stirring often, until the onion is very soft and golden brown, about 45 minutes. Set aside.

To cook the eggs:

- Crack 3 eggs into a cold sauté pan and add the remaining 1 tablespoon of butter. With a wooden spoon, stir the egg and butter mixture well, blending the yolks and whites to a uniform color. Do not stir vigorously: Whipping the eggs will ruin the consistency of the cooked eggs.
- Place the egg mixture over medium-high heat. Stir the eggs until the edges begin to curdle. Once the eggs start to coagulate, remove from the heat and stir the curds off the edges of the pan. Place the pan back on the heat and stir the eggs until they're the consistency of a thick custard. Add the chives and season with salt to taste. (Seasoning has to occur at the very end or the salt will break down the proteins, resulting in watery eggs.) Transfer the scrambled eggs to a metal bowl.

To assemble:

- Split and toast the bun and spread the Sriracha mayo on both halves. Pile the scrambled eggs onto the bottom half. Add the slice of cheddar to a hot nonstick sauté pan to melt it slightly, then arrange it on top of the eggs. Top with 1 tablespoon of the caramelized onions, cap with the bun top, and serve.

*Nutrition Info*

Calories: 234, Fat: 18g, Carbohydrates: 6 net grams, Protein: 24g

# VEGETARIAN BREAKFAST SANDWICHES

## Veggie Breakfast Sandwich

Prep/Cook Time: 15 minutes, Servings: 1

## *Ingredients*

- o 1 whole wheat English muffin, sliced in half and toasted (or two fairly small slices of bread, toasted)
- o 2 teaspoons mayonnaise
- o ½ ripe avocado, mashed
- o Salt and freshly ground black pepper
- o 1 large egg
- o ½ teaspoon water
- o 1 teaspoon butter or olive oil
- o 2 small slices of cheddar or Monterey Jack cheese (about ½ ounce, any other melty cheese will do)
- o 1 slice of ripe red tomato, if tomatoes are in season (optional)
- o Thinly sliced red onion
- o Several dashes of hot sauce (like Tabasco or Cholula)
- o Small handful arugula or sprouts

## Instructions

- To prepare your sandwiches, spread the mayonnaise over the lower half of your toasted muffin. Spread the mashed avocado over the other half, and sprinkle it with a few dashes of salt and pepper.
- Heat a medium non-stick skillet or well-seasoned cast iron skillet over medium-high heat. In a bowl, scramble the egg with the water and a few dashes of salt and pepper.
- Once the skillet is hot, add a pat of butter and swirl the pan to coat the bottom. Pour in the scrambled egg and immediately swirl the egg in the bottom of the pan to make an even layer.
- Immediately place your cheese in the center of the egg mixture as shown. Once the egg is set enough to fold over onto itself with a spatula (this could take 30 seconds to 1 minute), fold one side over the middle, then the opposite side over the middle. Repeat with the other two sides so you have a cute little egg and cheese envelope. Let it cook for another 15 to 30 seconds, until it's set enough that you can transfer it to a plate.
- Place the cooked egg on the mayo-covered bun. Top with a slice of tomato, if using. Add with several slices of red onion, a few dashes of hot sauce, and a little handful of arugula. Top it with the remaining bun, avocado side down.
- To slice it in half, insert a sharp knife into the center of the sandwich, and slice across to one edge. Repeat in the opposite direction. Serve warm! If you're making more sandwiches, reduce the stove temperature from medium-high to medium, as the pan only gets hotter the longer it's on the stove.

## Nutrition Info

Calories 210, Calories from Fat 400, Total Fat 45g, Saturated Fat, 25g, Cholesterol 205mg, Protein 41g

# Make Ahead Ham and Veggie Breakfast Sandwiches

Prep/Cook Time 50mins, Servings: 6 sandwiches

## Ingredients

- 1/2 tablespoon olive oil, plus more for oiling the pan
- 1/2 large onion, thinly sliced
- 2 cups packed baby spinach
- 10 large eggs
- 2 tablespoons cream or half and half
- 1/2 teaspoon fine sea salt
- 1/4 teaspoon fresh ground black pepper
- 2 tablespoons chopped fresh herbs, like chives, parsley or basil
- 6 slices ham, turkey, bacon or sausage patties, optional
- 6 slices cheese, like cheddar, provolone, or Swiss
- 6 English muffins or bread rolls

## Instructions

Make Eggs

- Position an oven rack in the middle of the oven and heat oven to 350 degrees F. Grease a 9-inch-by-13-inch baking dish or sheet pan (quarter sheet pan).

- Heat olive oil in a skillet over medium heat. Add the onions and cook until softened, about 5 minutes. Stir in the spinach and cook until wilted and bright green, 2 to 3 minutes. Set aside until warm, not hot.

- Meanwhile, whisk the eggs, cream, salt, pepper and fresh herbs together until blended. Stir in the cooked onions and spinach then pour into the prepared baking dish. Bake until the eggs look puffed and set, 25 to 35 minutes. (You can tell they are set when a knife can be inserted into the middle and comes out clean). Cool completely.

- While the eggs cool, cook the bacon or sausage (if using), toast the English muffins and slice or grate the cheese.

Assemble

- To assemble, chose the shape you want the eggs to be for the sandwiches. For perfect edges, use a round cookie cutter that's similar in size to the muffins to cut 6 egg patties. Save the leftover egg scrapes in a container in the fridge and enjoy as snacks or a breakfast later in the week. For no scrapes, make 6 rectangular egg patties. These will be larger than the muffins, but still work well in the sandwiches.

- Top the bottom half of each English muffin with an egg patty, meat (if using) and a slice of cheese. Finish with the muffin top.

Storing Sandwiches

- Wrap each breakfast sandwich tight in aluminum foil or freezer paper. Use a permanent marker to write the contents and date on the sandwich. Refrigerate up to 4 days or freeze up to 1 month. (We prefer refrigerating since freezing seems to pull out some additional moisture, but freezing is an excellent long-term solution).

Reheating Sandwiches

- Unwrap the sandwich and place on a microwave-safe plate. Cover with a damp paper towel. Microwave for 1 to 2 minutes, or until the cheese melts and the egg is warmed through.

- If you find you do not like the texture of microwaved bread, you can remove the bread from the sandwich and toast it. While it toasts, place the egg, meat and cheese on a microwave-safe plate. Cover with a damp paper towel. Microwave for 1 to 2 minutes, or until the cheese melts and the egg is warmed through. Reassemble the sandwich.

*Nutrition Info*

Calories 435, Protein 28 g, Carbohydrate 28 g, Dietary Fiber 2 g, Total Sugars 3 g, Total Fat 22 g, Saturated Fat 11 g, Cholesterol 358 mg, Sodium 1113 mg

# Vegan French Toast Breakfast Sandwiches

Prep/Cook Time: 30 min, Servings: Makes 4 Sandwiches

## *Ingredients*

For the French Toast:

- 8 slices vegan white bread, left out on the counter for about an hour to get a little stale
- 1 ½ cups just egg or follow your heart vegan egg
- 1 tbs oat milk
- 1 tbs maple syrup
- 2 tsp vanilla
- ½ tsp cinnamon
- 1/8 tsp salt
- 4 tbs vegan butter

Sandwich Fillings:

- Vegan Egg substitute of your choice, I used Just Egg, I needed about 1/3 bottle per sandwich, I also have a tofu "egg" recipe you can use from this recipe
- Vegan Breakfast sausage, vegan bacon, or vegan deli ham slices
- 4 slices vegan cheddar or other vegan cheese of your choice
- More butter, oil, or spray to cook the eggs with
- Extra maple syrup for serving!

## Instructions

- Whisk together vegan egg, oat milk, maple syrup, vanilla, cinnamon, & salt in a shallow flat container or pie dish.
- Heat a large pan over medium-high heat, I had mine at a 6 on my electric stove. Add 1 tbs butter.
- Dunk 2 pieces of bread into the egg mixture, making sure to evenly coat both sides, then add to the pan once butter is melted and hot. Cook 3-4 minutes on each side, set aside on a plate. Repeat until all bread is used.
- While the French toast is cooking, heat another large pan and cook up your vegan egg or tofu according to package or recipe.
- If you're using sausage, cook according to package instructions. Now assemble your sandwiches by loading them up equally with vegan egg, sausage, and cheese! Serve with warm maple syrup if desired.

## Nutrition Info

Calories: 190, Fat: 19g, Carbohydrates: 9g, Fiber: 2g, Protein: 13g

# Mediterranean Breakfast Sandwiches

## Ingredients

- 4 multigrain sandwich thins
- 4 teaspoons olive oil
- 1 tablespoon snipped fresh rosemary or 1/2 teaspoon dried rosemary, crushed
- 4 eggs
- 2 cups fresh baby spinach leaves
- 1 medium tomato, cut into 8 thin slices
- 4 tablespoons reduced-fat feta cheese
- ⅛ teaspoon kosher salt
- Freshly ground black pepper

## Instructions

- Preheat oven to 375 degrees F. Split sandwich thins; brush cut sides with 2 teaspoons of the olive oil. Place on baking sheet; toast in oven about 5 minutes or until edges are light brown and crisp.

- Meanwhile, in a large skillet heat the remaining 2 teaspoons olive oil and the rosemary over medium-high heat. Break eggs, one at a time, into skillet. Cook about 1 minute or until whites are set but yolks are still runny. Break yolks with spatula. Flip eggs; cook on other side until done. Remove from heat.
- Place the bottom halves of the toasted sandwich thins on four serving plates. Divide spinach among sandwich thins on plates. Top each with two of the tomato slices, an egg and 1 tablespoon of the feta cheese. Sprinkle with the salt and pepper. Top with the remaining sandwich thin halves.

*Nutrition Info*

242 calories; total fat 11.7g 18% DV; saturated fat 2.9g; cholesterol 214mg 71% DV; sodium 501mg 20% DV; potassium 144mg 4% DV; carbohydrates 25g

Prep/Cook Time 4 hours 40 minutes, Servings 6

## Ingredients

For the Spicy Cashew Cheese

- o 1 cup raw cashews, soaked in water 4 to 8 hours, drained and rinsed
- o 2 tablespoons vinegar-based hot sauce (such as Cholula), plus more, to taste
- o 2 tablespoons unsweetened and unflavored non-dairy milk, plus more as needed
- o 1/2 teaspoon salt

For the Eggy Chickpea Patties

- o 2/3 cup chickpea flour
- o 2 tablespoons nutritional yeast flakes
- o 1/2 teaspoon baking powder
- o 1/2 teaspoon ground cumin
- o 1/2 teaspoon paprika
- o 1/4 teaspoon turmeric

- o 1/4 teaspoon Kala namak (for eggy flavor, can substitute table salt)
- o 1/4 teaspoon black pepper
- o 1/2 cup water
- o 1 tablespoon soy sauce
- o 1 tablespoon olive oil (or high-heat oil of choice)

For the Sandwiches

- o 4 vegan English muffins, split and toasted
- o 1/2 batch tempeh bacon (optional)
- o 1/2 cup baby spinach
- o Additional fillings or sauces of choice, such as salsa, ketchup, sliced vegan cheese, avocado, etc.

## *Instructions*

To Make the Spicy Cashew Cheese

- Place all ingredients into the bowl of a food processor fitted with an s-blade. Blend until smooth.
- Taste-test the mixture and adjust the seasonings to your liking. Thin the mixture with additional milk if it seems too thick. Blend again.

To Make the Eggy Chickpea Patties

- Whisk the chickpea flour, nutritional yeast, baking powder, cumin, paprika, turmeric, kala namak and black pepper together in a small bowl.

- Whisk in the water and soy sauce.
- Coat the bottom of a medium skillet with olive oil and place it over medium heat.
- Give the oil a minute to heat up, then pour about 1/4 cup of batter into the skillet, making an approximately 3-inch patty. Repeat for as many patties as you can fit into the skillet without crowding.
- Cook the patties for 3 to 4 minutes, until bubbles form in the center, then flip and cook about 3 to 4 minutes more, until set and lightly browned.
- Remove the patties from the skillet and transfer them to a plate. Repeat the process until all of the batter is used.

To Assemble the Sandwiches

- Slather the inside of one or both halves of each muffin with the spicy cashew cheese, then layer and stuff with the eggy patties, tempeh bacon (if using), and spinach on the bottom halves, along with any additional fillings you choose.

- Serve.

*Nutrition Info*

Calories 468 Calories from Fat 158, Fat 17.5g, Saturated Fat 2.8g, Sodium 1189mg, Potassium 751mg, Carbohydrates 55.8g, Fiber 9.7g, Sugar 7.7g, Protein 21.8g44

## Roast Pork Sandwiches with Garlic Mayo

Prep/Cook Time: 1 hr 5 mins, Servings: 4

### Ingredients

- o   1 head garlic
- o   Coarse salt
- o   Extra-virgin olive oil
- o   1 red onion, halved lengthwise
- o   2 teaspoons Dijon mustard
- o   1/2 cup mayonnaise
- o   4 submarine rolls (10 to 12 inches long), cut in half horizontally
- o   20 to 24 thin slices roast pork
- o   Roasted fennel, chiles, and pitted olives (optional)
- o   16 thin slices provolone or fontina cheese

## Instructions

- Preheat oven to 375 degrees. Cut off and discard top 1/2 inch of garlic head. Season garlic with salt, drizzle with oil, and wrap snugly in foil. Roast until tender when squeezed, 50 to 55 minutes.
- Meanwhile, toss onion with just enough oil to coat, and roast on a rimmed baking sheet 40 to 45 minutes.
- When garlic is cool enough to handle, squeeze from skin; lightly mash with a fork. Stir in mustard and mayonnaise.
- Raise heat to broil. Spread garlic mayonnaise on bottom halves of rolls; top with pork. Top remaining halves with vegetables, then cheese. Broil open-faced until cheese is melted and bubbling, about 2 minutes, then sandwich rolls together.

## Nutrition Info

Calories 256, Total Fat 15g, Total Carbohydrate 16g, Sugars 9.5g, Protein 18.1g

# Cold Pork Roast Sandwiches

Prep/Cook Time: 10 mins, Servings: 4

## Ingredients

- 1/4 cup (60 ml) mayonnaise
- 1 tbsp (15 ml) whole-grain mustard
- 2 tbsp chopped fresh chives
- 8 slices crusty bread
- 12 thin slices cold pork roast (see recipe)
- 8 leaves Boston lettuce, or iceberg
- Salt and pepper

## Instructions

- In a bowl, combine the mayonnaise and mustard. Add the chives. Set aside.
- Toast the bread, if desired.
- Spread the mayonnaise mixture on the bread. Top with the pork slices and lettuce. Season with salt and pepper. Close the sandwiches.

## Nutrition Info

Calories: 403 Calories, Total Carbs: 16g, Fiber: 5.3g, Net Carbs: 7.3g, Protein: 40g, Fat: 40.21g

Prep/Cook Time 2 hrs 30 mins, Servings: 12

## *Ingredients*

Roast Pork

- o  4 lbs pork loin roast
- o  1/4 cup brown mustard
- o  4 tbsp Montreal Steak Seasoning*
- o  1 lb sliced Provolone aged or regular
- o  12 Kaiser rolls or the roll of your choice

Broccoli Rabe

- o  1 head broccoli rabe
- o  2 tbsp olive oil
- o  1 clove garlic diced

Roasted Red Peppers and Long hots

- o  2 large red peppers
- o  1 tablespoon olive oil
- o  sea salt and pepper to season

Make Your Own Montreal Steak Seasoning

- o  2 tablespoons paprika
- o  2 tablespoons cracked black pepper
- o  2 tablespoons kosher salt
- o  1 tablespoon granulated garlic

- 1 tablespoon granulated onion
- 1 tablespoon crushed coriander
- 1 tablespoon dill
- 1 tablespoon crushed red pepper flakes

## *Instructions*

Pork Roast

- Coat top side of pork roast with brown or deli mustard, rub into meat.
- Sprinkle a liberal amount of Montreal Steak Seasoning over the mustard, covering the top completely.
- Place meat in 350 F degree oven (177 C), add a little water to the bottom of the pan and roast the pork loin for about two hours or until a meat thermometer reads 150 F (66 C) degrees. (the temp will rise 10 degrees as it sits)
- After the Pork has cooled completely cut it into thin slices to re-heat in the au jus.
- Add some water to all of the meat drippings and use this as your base for the pork au jus.

Broccoli Rabe

- Wash and trim the broccoli rabe removing any bad leaves and cutting off the stems, leaving only the leaves and flowers.
- Place the broccoli rabe into a pan with water and allow to boil until the broccoli rabe is tender. (do not use a full pot of water, use just enough to cook)

- Drain Broccoli rabe and saute in olive oil with chopped garlic, sea salt and pepper to taste.

Roasted Red Peppers and Long Hots
- Wash peppers, and cut down the center removing all the seed and membranes.
- Slice the red peppers about 3/8 of an inch thick (1 cm)
- Coat with olive oil and season with sea salt and black pepper
- Roast in 350 degree oven for 20-25 minutes
- Keep the peppers separate during the process, otherwise the long hots will make everything hot!

Make Your Own Montreal Beef Seasoning
- Combine paprika, crushed black pepper, kosher salt, granulated garlic, granulated onion, crushed coriander, dill, and crushed red pepper flakes, mix well.

Assembly
- Reheat the sliced pork in the au jus you saved from the pan
- place slices of roast pork on kaiser roll, add provolone, broccoli rabe and roasted red peppers.
- serve with extra au jus and long hots!

*Nutrition Info*

Calories: 577kcal, Carbohydrates: 38g, Protein: 51g, Fat: 23g, Saturated Fat: 9g, Cholesterol: 121mg, Sodium: 1893mg, Potassium: 865mg

Prep/Cook Time 1 hr 5 mins, Servings: 8

## Ingredients

- o  2 lb Pork loin
- o  1 tablespoon Cooking Oil
- o  Fresh Ground Pepper
- o  Salt
- o  1 medium Onion (see notes)
- o  1/2 pound Provolone Cheese (sliced)
- o  Crusty French Bread (enough for 8 servings)

Stone Ground Honey Mustard

- o  1/4 cup Mayo
- o  2 tablespoons Stone Ground Mustard
- o  1 tablespoon Honey
- o  1/8 teaspoon fresh Ground Pepper

## Instructions

- •  Preheat oven to 350 degrees.

- Rub the pork loin with cooking oil and dust with salt and pepper, or your desired seasonings.
- Place in the oven and roast until digital thermometer reads 145 degrees, approximately 1 hour.
- While pork is roasting saute, grill, or caramelized onions. (see note)
- Remove pork loin from oven and let rest for 10 minutes.
- While pork loin is resting slice open the French Bread and lightly toast the interior until beginning to brown. This can be done in toaster, in a hot skillet, or under the broiler.
- Thinly slice the pork and place on the French bread, then top with Provolone cheese. With the sandwich lying open, place briefly under the broiler set on High until cheese is melted.
- Remove from the broiler and top with onions and honey mustard and serve immediately.

Stone Ground Honey Mustard

- Prepare the honey mustard while pork is roasting by combining mayo, mustard, honey, and ground pepper in a small bowl.

Notes : You can rub the pork loin with your favorite seasonings if desired.

*Nutrition Info :* Calories: 322

# Pulled Pork Sandwiches

Prep/Cook Time: 6 hr 45 min, Servings: 12 sandwiches

## *Ingredients*

For the Pork:

- o 6 tablespoons paprika
- o 3 tablespoons granulated sugar
- o Scant tablespoon onion powder
- o Kosher salt and coarsely ground pepper
- o 1 10-to-12-pound boneless pork shoulder or Boston butt, rinsed and dried
- o 12 soft hamburger buns, split
- o Coleslaw, for serving

For the Barbecue Sauce:

- o 2 cups ketchup
- o 1/4 cup packed light brown sugar
- o 1/4 cup granulated sugar
- o Freshly ground pepper
- o 1 1/2 teaspoons onion powder
- o 1 1/2 teaspoons dry mustard
- o 2 tablespoons fresh lemon juice

- o  2 tablespoons Worcestershire sauce
- o  1/2 cup apple cider vinegar
- o  2 tablespoons light corn syrup

## *Instructions*

- If using a gas grill, preheat to high on one side; put soaked wood chips in a smoker box. Once smoking, reduce the heat to maintain a temperature of 275 degrees F and cook the pork, covered, on the cooler side of the grill.
- Rub the pork
- Make the Neelys' go-to barbecue seasoning: Mix the paprika, sugar and onion powder in a bowl. Transfer 3 tablespoons seasoning to a separate bowl, add 2 tablespoons salt and 3 tablespoons pepper, and massage onto the pork. Cover with plastic wrap and refrigerate at least 2 hours or up to 1 day. (Reserve the remaining barbecue seasoning.)
- Prepare the wood chips: Soak 6 cups wood chips in water, about 15 minutes, then drain. Don't oversoak, or the wood will snuff out the fire.
- Light the grill: Fill a smoker or kettle grill with charcoal and light. (Pat uses lighter fluid; you can also use a chimney starter.) When the coals are mostly white, spread them out with tongs. Spread 1/2 cup of the wood chips over the coals (use 1 cup for a kettle grill). The temperature of the grill should be about 275 degrees F.
- Cook the pork: Place the pork fat-side down on a rack in the smoker or on the grill. Cover and cook, rotating

the pork every hour or so, until a thermometer inserted into the center registers 165 degrees F, about 6 hours total.

- Feed the grill: As the pork cooks, add more charcoal and wood chips to keep the temperature between 250 degrees F and 275 degrees F and to maintain the smoke level.
- Make the sauce: Meanwhile, mix the ketchup, 1 cup water, both sugars, 1 1/2 teaspoons pepper, the onion and mustard powders, lemon juice, Worcestershire sauce, vinegar, corn syrup and 1 tablespoon of the reserved barbecue seasoning in a saucepan over high heat. Bring to a boil, stirring, then reduce the heat to low and simmer, uncovered, stirring occasionally, at least 2 hours. Let cool, then reheat on the grill when ready to use.
- Shred the pork: Transfer the pork to a rimmed baking sheet (you'll want to catch all the flavorful juices) and let stand until cool enough to handle. Shred into bite-size pieces, pile on a platter and pour any juices from the baking sheet on top.
- Make the sandwiches: Mound the pork on bun bottoms, paint with a little barbecue sauce, top with slaw and cover with the bun tops. The best sandwich ever!

*Nutrition Info*

Calories 212 Calories from Fat 110, Fat 16.5g, Carbohydrates 3g, Protein 22.5g

## The Best Fried Chicken Sandwiches

Prep/Cook Time : 4 hours 50 minutes, Servings: 4 servings

### Ingredients
Chicken
- o 4 boneless skinless chicken thighs
- o 1/2 cup buttermilk
- o 1 teaspoon hot sauce
- o 1 teaspoon plus 1 tablespoon kosher salt
- o 1 1/2 cups all-purpose flour
- o 1 tablespoon kosher salt
- o 1 teaspoon freshly cracked black pepper
- o 2 teaspoons garlic powder
- o 2 teaspoons smoked paprika
- o canola oil for frying

Sauce

- o 1/2 cup mayonnaise
- o 1 teaspoon smoked paprika

- o 1 teaspoon hot sauce

Assembly
- o 4 brioche burger buns toasted
- o 1 cup thinly sliced cabbage
- o bread and butter pickles

## *Instructions*

- Add chicken, buttermilk, hot sauce, and 1 teaspoon kosher salt to a large resealable bag and refrigerate at least 4 hours or up to overnight.
- Heat 1 ½ inches of canola oil in a dutch oven or large pot to 350 degrees.
- In a wide bowl, combine flour, remaining salt, pepper, garlic powder, smoked paprika, and canola oil. Remove the chicken from the buttermilk marinade and dip each piece in the flour mixture until well coated.
- Fry two piece of chicken at a time until golden brown and cooked through, about 4 minutes per side. Rest the cooked chicken on paper towels to cool.
- Make the sauce by combining all sauce ingredients in a small bowl.
- Assemble sandwiches by spreading the open sides of the toasted buns with sauce. Top the bottom bun with fried chicken, pickles, lettuce, and the top bun.

## *Nutrition Info*

Calories 693 Calories from Fat 333, Fat 37g, Saturated Fat 14g, Cholesterol 257mg, Sodium 2237mg, Potassium 475mg, Carbohydrates 84g, Fiber 3g, Sugar 6g, Protein 38g76%

# Crispy Chicken Sandwich

## *Ingredients*

Brine

- o  1 quart water
- o  ¼ cup kosher salt
- o  ¼ cup sugar

Sandwich

- o  4 chicken breasts boneless, skinless
- o  4 sesame seed buns
- o  4 Tablespoons butter
- o  2 cups shredded iceberg lettuce
- o  ¼ cup mayonnaise
- o  dill pickle slices
- o  3 quarts vegetable oil for frying

Batter

- o  1 cup all-purpose flour
- o  ¾ cup Argo® Corn Starch
- o  1 teaspoon Argo® Baking Powder
- o  4 teaspoons ground black pepper
- o  2 teaspoons kosher salt
- o  1 teaspoon garlic powder
- o  1 teaspoon onion powder
- o  1 teaspoon paprika

- ○ ½ teaspoon cayenne pepper
- ○ ¾ cup cold water

## Instructions

Brine

- Pound chicken to ½" - ¾" thick (just to make sure it's even). Combine all brine ingredients in a large bowl until sugar/salt are dissolved. Add chicken, cover and refrigerate 1 hour.

Chicken

- Combine flour, corn starch, baking powder and seasonings in a bowl. Remove ¾ cup of this flour mixture and place in a shallow pan (this is the dry dredge).
- Add ¾ cup cold water to the remaining flour mixture and whisk until smooth. *see note
- Heat oil over medium heat to 350°F in a Dutch oven or deep pan.
- Remove chicken breasts from the brine; pat dry with paper towels. Discard the brine.
- Dip the chicken breasts into dry mixture, shaking off any excess and then into the batter ensuring it's coated on both sides. Allow excess batter to drip off. Dip back into the dry mixture to gently coat.
- Carefully place chicken in the hot oil (ensuring it stays at 350°F). Cook until the chicken coating is a deep golden brown and the internal temperature reaches

165°F, about 3-4 minutes per side (depending on thickness).

- Remove from oil and place chicken on a paper towel lined plate to drain.

To Assemble

- Butter each sesame seed bun and toast under the broiler just until golden.
- Spread 2 tablespoons mayonnaise over the bottom of each roll. Top with lettuce, pickles, and crispy chicken.

*Nutrition Info*

Calories: 861, Carbohydrates: 46g, Protein: 54g, Fat: 51g, Saturated Fat: 28g, Cholesterol: 181mg, Sodium: 1249mg, Potassium: 971mg, Fiber: 2g, Sugar: 3g

# Cafe Style Grilled Chicken Sandwiches

Prep/Cook Time: 55 mins, Servings: 4

## Ingredients

- 2 breast half, bone and skin removed (blank)s skinless, boneless chicken breast halves
- ¼ cup olive oil
- 2 tablespoons white wine vinegar
- 1 lemon, juiced
- 1 tablespoon garlic and herb seasoning blend (such as Mrs. Dash®)
- 1 teaspoon ground black pepper
- 4 sprigs fresh dill, chopped
- 2 tablespoons butter
- 2 tablespoons olive oil
- ⅛ teaspoon garlic powder
- ⅛ teaspoon salt
- 8 thick slices French bread
- 2 tablespoons mayonnaise, or to taste
- 4 slices tomato
- 4 large leaf (blank)s lettuce leaves

## Instructions

- Preheat grill to medium-high heat.
- Prick chicken breasts all over with a fork. Place chicken breasts, 1/4 cup olive oil, white wine vinegar, lemon juice, garlic and herb seasoning, ground black pepper, and chopped fresh dill in a bowl. Stir to coat chicken breasts completely. Let stand for 10 minutes.

48

- Remove chicken breasts from marinade, discard marinade, and grill chicken for 10 to 15 minutes on each side, or until juices run clear and an instant-read meat thermometer inserted into the thickest part of a breast reads at least 160 degrees F (70 degrees C). Remove from grill; let stand for 5 minutes. Cut chicken breasts in half.
- Melt butter and 2 tablespoons olive oil in a skillet over medium-high heat. Sprinkle garlic powder and salt over butter and oil. Add French bread slices to the pan and toast until golden brown on one side, about 3 minutes; remove from pan.
- For sandwich assembly, place one slice of French bread with toasted side down onto a serving plate. Spread mayonnaise on bread; top with a slice of tomato, salt and ground black pepper to taste, half a grilled chicken breast, and lettuce. Spread untoasted side of another slice of bread with mayonnaise and place on top to make a sandwich.

*Nutrition Info*

553 calories; protein 20.3g; carbohydrates 42.6g; fat 34.1g; cholesterol 48.3mg sodium 637.2mg

# DIY Popeyes Buttermilk Fried Chicken Sandwich

Prep/Cook Time: 30 minutes, Servings: 4

## Ingredients

For the chicken marinade

- 2 boneless skinless chicken breasts
- 1 cup buttermilk
- 1 teaspoon EACH paprika garlic powder, black pepper, salt

For Breading

- 1 cup flour
- ½ cup corn starch
- 1 tablespoon EACH paprika garlic powder, onion powder, cayenne pepper (for spicy)
- 1 teaspoon EACH salt & pepper

Spicy mayo

- ½ cup mayo
- 1 teaspoon hot sauce
- 1 teaspoon or cajun or taco seasoning 1/2 tsp

TO ASSEMBLE

- 4 medium-sized brioche buns
- Mayonnaise

- ○ Sliced pickles
- ○ 3-4 cups canola oil for frying

*Instructions*

To Marinate Chicken

- Pound chicken breasts in between two pieces of parchment paper or plastic wrap. Cut each chicken breast in half crosswise to make 2 small pieces of chicken about the same size as the bun.
- In a large bowl, buttermilk, paprika, garlic powder, salt & black pepper. Add the chicken to the mix and place in the fridge to marinate up to 24 hours or use right away.

To Cook Chicken

- Heat oil in a large heavy-duty skillet or pot on medium temperature or until the temperature reaches 350F.
- In a medium shallow bowl, whisk the flour, cornstarch, and spices. Drizzle 2-3 tablespoons of the buttermilk batter into the flour mixture and mix it through with a fork.
- Working with 1 piece at a time, dredge chicken the flour mixture and press flour on the top chicken to form a thick crust. Transfer chicken to hot oil and fry for 3-5 minutes per side or until the outside is crispy and golden and the internal temperature reaches 165F.

To Assemble

- Melt 1 tablespoon butter in a large saucepan and toast buns face down until golden and crisp. Whisk all the ingredients for the mayo in a small bowl and spread a generous layer of mayo on each bun. Top with pickles and chicken. Enjoy hot!

*Nutrition Info*

Calories 221, Fat 20g, Protein 27g, Total Carbs 7g, Net Carbs 4g, Fiber 3g
Sugar 3g

# Buttermilk-Fried Chicken Sandwich

Prep/Cook Time: 1:04, 8 servings

## *Ingredients*

Buttermilk Marinade
- o   2 cups buttermilk (480 mL)
- o   1 teaspoon salt
- o   1 teaspoon black pepper
- o   ½ teaspoon cayenne pepper
- o   8 boneless, skinless chicken thighs

Dill Dressing
- o   1 ½ cups plain greek yogurt (425 g)
- o   3 tablespoons fresh dill, chopped
- o   1 teaspoon garlic powder
- o   2 tablespoons lemon juice
- o   ¼ cup grated parmesan cheese (30 g)

Seasoned Flour
- o   2 cups all-purpose flour (250 g)
- o   1 tablespoon salt
- o   2 teaspoons black pepper
- o   1 ½ teaspoons cayenne pepper
- o   1 tablespoon garlic powder
- o   peanut or vegetable oil, for frying

For Serving
- o   softened butter, for buns
- o   8 brioche burger buns
- o   1 head butter lettuce
- o   2 tomatoes, sliced

## Instructions

- Make the buttermilk marinade: In a medium bowl, combine the buttermilk, salt, pepper, and cayenne. Toss in the chicken thighs in the marinade to coat. Marinate for at least 1 hour in the refrigerator, or overnight.
- Make the dill dressing: In a small bowl, combine the yogurt, dill, garlic powder, lemon juice, and Parmesan cheese. Cover and let sit for at least 1 hour in the refrigerator to chill.
- Make the seasoned flour: In a medium bowl, combine the flour, salt, pepper, cayenne, and garlic powder. Dip the marinated chicken in the flour mixture until the chicken is completely covered.
- Heat the oil in a deep pot until it reaches 350°F (180°C). Do not fill more than halfway with oil. Carefully fry the chicken for 7 minutes, or until cooked through.
- The internal temperature should reach 165°F (75°C), and the chicken should be golden brown and crispy. Drain on a paper towel–lined plate or wire rack.
- Heat a large skillet over medium heat. Butter the cut sides of the burger buns, then toast on the hot skillet until browned and crisp. Build the sandwiches with the toasted buns, lettuce, fried chicken, tomato slices, and dill dressing.
- Enjoy!

## Nutrition Info

Calories 578 Fat 13g Carbs 77g Fiber 3g Sugar 13g Protein 34g

# TURKEY SANDWICHES

## Awesome Turkey Sandwich

Prep/Cook Time: 10 mins, Servings: 1

### Ingredients

- o 2 slices whole wheat bread, toasted
- o 1 tablespoon mayonnaise
- o 2 teaspoons Dijon-style prepared mustard
- o 3 slices smoked turkey breast
- o 2 tablespoons guacamole
- o ½ cup mixed salad greens
- o ¼ cup bean sprouts
- o ¼ avocado - peeled, pitted and sliced
- o 3 ounces Colby-Monterey Jack cheese, sliced
- o 2 slices tomato

### Instructions

- Spread mayonnaise on one slice of toast, then spread mustard on the other. Arrange the sliced turkey on one side. Spread guacamole over the turkey. Pile on the salad greens, bean sprouts, avocado and cheese. Finish with tomato slices, then place the remaining slice of toast on top.

### Nutrition Info

804.2 calories; protein 37.9g; carbohydrates 41.4g; fat 56.6g; cholesterol 124.2mg

# California-Style Turkey Sandwich

Prep/Cook Time: 10 min, Servings: 4 serving

## Ingredients

- 1/4 cup low-fat mayonnaise
- 1 tablespoon chopped fresh parsley
- 2 teaspoons chopped fresh thyme
- 1 (8-ounce) package Hillshire Farm(R) Deli Select(R) Oven Roasted Turkey Breast
- 8 slices sourdough bread or 4 sourdough buns, sliced in 1/2
- 1 avocado, halved, pitted, peeled and sliced
- 4 slices Monterey Jack cheese
- Fresh ground pepper

## Instructions

- In a small bowl, combine the mayonnaise, parsley, and thyme. Mix until well combined. Spread some mayonnaise onto 1 slice of bread. Add 1/4 of the Hillshire Farm(R) Deli Select(R) Oven Roasted Turkey Breast to each slice. Add 1/4 of the sliced avocado. Top with Monterey Jack cheese, season with a bit of pepper and top with a slice of bread. Repeat with the remaining ingredients.

## Nutrition Info

Calories: 351kcal, Carbohydrates: 8g, Protein: 31g, Fat: 20g, Saturated Fat: 5g, Cholesterol: 128mg

Prep/Cook Time 5 minutes, Servings: 8 servings

## Ingredients

- 4 cups cooked turkey, white and dark meat
- 1 cup pickle relish
- 1/2 cup mayo or Miracle Whip
- 1 teaspoon celery salt
- 1 teaspoon black pepper

## Instructions

- Leftover turkey, both white and dark meat goes into the bowl of a food processor.
- Add sweet pickle relish and mayo or my guys love Miracle Whip.
- Add celery salt & black pepper.
- Cover and pulse until turkey is chopped fine and all is combined.
- Store in an airtight container in the refrigerator.

- Makes delicious sandwiches or serve with your favorite crackers!

### Nutrition Info

Calories: 296 Total Fat: 17g Saturated Fat: 4g Unsaturated Fat: 13g Cholesterol: 93mg Sodium: 584mg Carbohydrates: 11g Sugar: 9g Protein: 23g

Prep/Cook Time 10 min, Servings 4

## Ingredients

- o  1/3 cup mayonnaise or salad dressing
- o  1 tablespoon chopped fresh or 1 teaspoon dried basil leaves
- o  1/4 teaspoon garlic powder
- o  8 slices sourdough bread, 1/2 inch thick
- o  8 large spinach leaves
- o  1/2 lb sliced oven roasted turkey breast
- o  1/2 cup chopped drained roasted red bell peppers (from 7-oz jar)

## Instructions

- In small bowl, mix mayonnaise, basil and garlic powder. Spread on one side of each bread slice.
- Layer spinach, turkey and bell peppers on 4 slices of bread. Top with remaining bread.

Tips

- You can use any type of bread for these cold sandwiches, including pita breads, kaiser rolls or bagels, if you like.
- You may need more (or fewer) spinach leaves depending on the size of the leaves you use. Just be sure the spinach leaves cover the bread slice.

### *Nutrition Info*

Calories 420, Calories from Fat 160, Total Fat 18g, Saturated Fat 3g, Trans Fat 1/2g, Protein 25g

# Hot Brown Turkey Sandwiches

Prep/Cook Time: 35 min, Servings: 4 servings

## Ingredients

- 5 slices bacon
- 1 small onion, chopped
- 2 tablespoons all-purpose flour
- 1 1/4 cups milk
- 1 1/4 cups low-sodium chicken broth
- 1 1/4 cups shredded Muenster or Monterey Jack cheese
- Kosher salt and freshly ground pepper
- 4 thick slices white bread, toasted
- Dijon mustard, for spreading
- 1 tomato, sliced
- 3 cups shredded or sliced roast turkey or rotisserie chicken
- 1/4 cup chopped fresh parsley

## Instructions

- Preheat the broiler. Cook the bacon in a large skillet over medium heat until crisp, about 10 minutes. Transfer to a paper towel-lined plate. Pour out all but about 1 tablespoon fat from the skillet.
- Make the gravy: Add the onion to the skillet and cook, stirring, until soft, about 3 minutes. Add the flour and cook, stirring, 1 more minute. Increase the heat to medium high, add the milk and chicken broth and bring to a boil, stirring. Reduce the heat to medium low and simmer, stirring, until slightly thickened, about 6

61

minutes. Remove from the heat and stir in 1 cup cheese. Season with salt and pepper.

- Arrange the bread on a baking sheet. Spread each slice with mustard, then drizzle with some of the gravy and top with the sliced tomato. Toss the turkey with the remaining gravy in the skillet. Divide the turkey evenly among the bread slices, then sprinkle with the remaining 1/4 cup cheese. Broil until golden, about 2 minutes.
- Crumble the bacon over the sandwiches; sprinkle with the parsley.

### *Nutrition Info*

Calories 222, Fat 23g, Saturated Fat 11g, Cholesterol 162mg, Sodium 1692mg, Potassium 969mg, Carbohydrates 13g

## Crispy Fish Sandwich

Prep/Cook Time: 30 minutes, Servings: 4

### Ingredients

- 1 small red onion, thinly sliced into rounds
- 4 oz. bread-and-butter pickles, plus 1/2 cup brine
- 3/4 cup mayonnaise
- 1/3 cup chopped dill
- 2 tsp. hot sauce
- 1 tsp. freshly ground black pepper
- 2 tsp. fresh lemon juice, plus wedges for serving
- 1 Tbsp. kosher salt, divided
- 2 large eggs, lightly beaten
- 1 1/2 cups panko (Japanese breadcrumbs)
- 1/2 cup all-purpose flour
- 2 flounder fillets (about 2/3 lb. total), cut in half crosswise on a diagonal
- 2/3 cup vegetable oil
- 3 cups shredded iceberg lettuce
- 8 slices Pullman bread
- 1 cup potato chips, plus more for serving

### Instructions

- Combine onion, pickles, and pickle brine in a small bowl.

63

- Mix mayonnaise, dill, hot sauce, pepper, 2 tsp. lemon juice, and 1/2 tsp. salt in another small bowl.
- Place eggs, panko, and flour in 3 separate shallow medium bowls. Season each fish fillet with 1/2 tsp. salt. Working one at a time, dredge fish in flour, shaking off excess. Coat evenly with egg, allowing excess to drip back into bowl. Coat with panko, pressing to adhere. Transfer fish to a plate.
- Heat oil in a large skillet over medium. Cook fish until breading is golden brown and cooked through, 2–3 minutes per side. Transfer fish to a paper towel-lined plate. Season fillets with 1/2 tsp. salt total.
- Spread 1 heaping Tbsp. mayonnaise mixture on one side of each slice of bread. Pile each bottom slice with 3/4 cup lettuce, 1 fish fillet, a small handful of potato chips, and 1/4 cup onion mixture. Close sandwich with second slice of bread, mayo side down, and push down lightly to crush potato chips. Transfer to a platter. Repeat with remaining sandwiches. Serve with lemon wedges and more potato chips alongside.
- Do Ahead: Pickled onions and dill sauce can be made 1 day ahead. Cover and chill.

*Nutrition Info*

Calories: 67kcal, Carbohydrates: 3g, Sodium: 474mg

# Seafood Salad Sandwiches

## Ingredients

- 1 1/2 cups chopped cooked seafood, such as crabmeat, shrimp or lobster
- 1/2 cup mayonnaise or salad dressing
- 1/4 teaspoon salt
- 1/4 teaspoon pepper
- 1 medium celery stalk, chopped (1/2 cup)
- 1 small onion, chopped (1/4 cup)
- 4 hot dog buns, split

## Instructions

- Mix all ingredients except buns.
- Fill buns with seafood mixture. Tuna Salad Filling: Substitute 1 can (9 ounces) tuna, drained, for the seafood. Stir in 1 teaspoon lemon juice. Chicken Salad Filling: Substitute 1 1/2 cups chopped cooked chicken or turkey for the seafood.

Tips

- Sliced cantaloupe and a mixture of red and green grapes would be a quick choice to serve with these easy sandwiches.
- For a more elegant presentation, serve the seafood, tuna or chicken salad filling on tender, flaky croissants

purchased from your favorite bakery or the freezer section of your grocery store.

*Nutrition Info*

Calories 375 Calories from Fat 225 Total Fat 25 g Saturated Fat 4 g Cholesterol 80 mg Sodium 710 mg Potassium 280 mg Total Carbohydrate 24 g, Protein 15 g

# Warm Seafood Sandwiches

Prep/Cook Time, Serves : 4

## Ingredients

- 1/4 cup plus 2 tablespoons extra-virgin olive oil 1/4 teaspoon crushed red pepper 1/2 pound cleaned small squid, cut into 1/2-inch rings 1 pound mussels, scrubbed and debearded 1 1/2 pounds littleneck clams, scrubbed 1/2 cup water One 24-inch baguette (10 ounces), ends trimmed 2 tablespoons fresh lemon juice 1 tablespoon chopped flat-leaf parsley Salt and freshly ground pepper

## Instructions

- In a large, deep skillet, heat 3 tablespoons of the olive oil until shimmering. Add the crushed red pepper and cook over high heat for 20 seconds to season the oil. Add the squid and cook, stirring, until opaque, about 1 minute. Using a slotted spoon, transfer the squid to a plate.
- Add the mussels, clams and water to the skillet, cover and cook over high heat, stirring occasionally, until the shells open, 2 to 3 minutes for the mussels and 5 to 8 minutes for the clams. Transfer the mussels and clams to a large bowl as they open. Remove the mussels and clams from their shells and rinse briefly to remove any grit. On a work surface, coarsely chop the mussels, clams and squid.

- Using a serrated knife, cut the baguette almost in half lengthwise, leaving one side attached. Scoop out the soft, white bread from the center of the baguette and tear it into 1/2-inch pieces.
- Wipe out the skillet, add 1 tablespoon of olive oil and heat until shimmering. Add the bread pieces and cook over moderate heat, stirring constantly, until golden and crisp, about 5 minutes. Add the seafood, lemon juice, parsley and the remaining 2 tablespoons of olive oil; season with salt and pepper. Spoon the filling onto the baguette, cut it crosswise into 4 pieces and serve.

### Nutrition Info

Calories 358, Total Fat 15.6g, Saturated Fat 5.6g, Protein 45.4g

# Grilled Seafood Sandwich Roll

Prep/Cook Time: 15 mins, Servings: 4

## Ingredients

- 1 Tbsp oil
- 1 lobster tail approx 6 oz
- 16 shrimp - medium to large size
- 1 c cook crab meat - picked over for shells
- 1/2 c mayonnaise - real mayo and not miracle whip
- 1/4 c shredded cheddar cheese - medium or sharp
- 3 Tbsp chopped red or green onion - your choice
- 1/4 c chopped celery
- 1/4 c chopped cucumber
- 1/2 tsp dried dill weed
- 1 Tbsp lemon juice - fresh is best if you have it
- 1/2 tsp salt
- 1 Tbsp melted butter
- 4 hot dog buns
- crisp lettuce
- 1 dash(es) hot sauce - if desired

## Instructions

- Place the lobster and the shrimp in a bowl and pour oil over all. Mix with hands until the seafood is coated.
- Place the lobster and shrimp on a hot grill and cook until done.
- Remove from grill and cool.
- When cooled, removed shells.

- Chop the lobster and shrimp into small pieces and place in medium bowl.
- Add crab and stir to mix.
- Add remaining ingredients except butter, buns, lettuce and hot sauce and mix well.
- Add mayonnaise until you get a good coating but do not saturate. Use more mayo if you need to.
- Cover and chill on ice or overnight in the fridge.
- Just before serving lightly brush the buns with butter and toast in a skillet.
- Line the buns with lettuce and then heap with the seafood mix and top with a dash of hot sauce if desired.

## Nutrition Info

Calories: 324kcal, Carbohydrates: 23g, Protein: 43g

# Crab Salad (Seafood Salad)

Prep/Cook Time: 10 minutes, Servings: 4 servings

## Ingredients

- 1 pound imitation crab krab meat
- 1 shallot minced (you can use red onion if you need)
- 1/2 cup mayonnaise
- 1/2 cup celery minced
- 1/2 teaspoon paprika
- 1/2 teaspoon dill
- 1/4 teaspoon Kosher salt
- 1/4 teaspoon black pepper

## Instructions

In a large bowl add all the ingredients together gently, stirring until well coated.

Refrigerate for an hour before serving.

## Nutrition Info

310 calories, Calories: 310g, Carbohydrates: 21g, Protein: 6g, Fat: 21g, Saturated Fat: 3g, Cholesterol: 24mg, Sodium: 971mg, Potassium: 53mg, Fiber: 1g, Sugar: 5g

# Oven-Fried Fish Sandwiches

Prep/Cook Time: 30 minutes, Servings: 4

## Ingredients

- 3/4 lb mild white fish fillets (tilapia, catfish)
- 1 large egg
- 1 tablespoon milk
- 1 cup dry breadcrumbs
- Salt and freshly ground black pepper
- Vegetable oil
- Leaf lettuce
- 4 slices cheddar cheese
- 4 soft sandwich rolls

For the tartar sauce (see notes):

- 1/4 cup mayonnaise
- 1/2 tablespoon sweet pickle relish (well-drained)
- 1/2 teaspoon Dijon-style mustard
- 2 teaspoons freshly squeezed lemon juice
- 2 teaspoons sweet onion, minced or grated

## Instructions

- Preheat the oven to 425°F and coat a shallow baking pan with nonstick spray.
- Whisk the egg and milk together in a shallow dish.
- Spread the breadcrumbs on a plate add 1 teaspoon of salt, a few grinds of black pepper and combine well.

- Drizzle the seasoned breadcrumbs with 1-1/2 tablespoons of vegetable oil and use your fingertips to distribute it through the mixture.
- Cut the fish fillets into 4 evenly-sized pieces.
- Dip the fish fillets in the egg mixture, then press them gently into the breadcrumbs to be sure they're well coated.
- Arrange the fillets on the prepared baking sheet and bake until the fish flakes easily and the coating is crisp and golden, 10 to 12 minutes.
- While the fish is cooking, make the tartar sauce by combining the mayonnaise, relish, mustard, lemon juice and onion in a small mixing bowl.
- Once the fish is crispy and cooked through, top each fillet with a slice of cheese and return to the oven just long enough for the cheese to melt.
- To serve, place some lettuce on the bottom half of each roll and top with a piece of fish and a spoonful of tartar sauce.

## Nutrition Info

Calories: 533Total Fat: 26g Saturated Fat: 9g Unsaturated Fat: 15g Cholesterol: 129mg Sodium: 735mg Carbohydrates: 37g Fiber: 2g Sugar: 1g Protein: 37g

# Seafood Sandwich

Prep/Cook Time: 50 mins, Servings: 2

## Ingredient

- o 1 (8 ounce) package imitation crab or lobster meat
- o ¼ cup mayonnaise
- o 1 tablespoon finely chopped red onion
- o 1 teaspoon lemon juice
- o ¼ teaspoon OLD BAY® Seasoning
- o 1 tablespoon butter, softened
- o 2 roll (blank)s hot dog buns

## Instructions

- In a medium bowl, flake the crabmeat, and mix in mayonnaise, onion, lemon juice and Old Bay seasoning. Cover and refrigerate for 30 minutes to allow the flavors to mingle.
- Spread butter on the inside of the hot dog buns, and toast under the broiler. Fill buns with the crab salad, and serve.

## Nutrition Info

478 calories; protein 13g 26% DV; carbohydrates 39.7g 13% DV; fat 30g 46% DV; cholesterol 48.1mg

Prep/Cook Time: 26 min, Servings: 4 servings

## Ingredients

- Grapeseed oil, for frying
- 2 1/2 pounds fresh flounder fillets
- 3 tablespoons seafood seasoning, plus more for sprinkling
- 2 cups all-purpose flour
- 2 cups panko bread crumbs
- 3 eggs beaten
- Remoulade sauce, recipe follows
- 1 large French baguette, cut into 4 servings
- 12 tomato slices
- 8 romaine leaves, chiffonade
- 1 small red onion, sliced thin

Remoulade Sauce:

- 1 teaspoon hot relish (recommended: Amish or Indian)
- 2 tablespoons capers
- 2 tablespoons Dijon mustard
- 2 teaspoons chopped fresh tarragon leaves
- 1/2 teaspoon chopped anchovies
- Freshly ground black pepper
- 2 teaspoons Worcestershire sauce
- 1/2 lemon, juiced
- 1 teaspoon hot sauce
- 1 1/2 cups mayonnaise

## Instructions

- 
- Preheat oil in saute pan.
- Wash off fillets and pat dry with a towel. Lightly sprinkle with seafood seasoning on both sides.
- In 3 separate bowls, place flour mixed with 3 tablespoons seafood seasoning. panko and 3 beaten eggs.
- Dredge fillets into flour, egg and then panko. Add fish to oil and fry until golden brown, about 4 to 6 minutes. Remove to a paper towel lined platter.
- Spread remoulade sauce on both sides of toasted bread with a rubber spatula. Layer some romaine on the bottom, then top with fish, sliced tomato, red onion and then finally, a little more romaine on top. Add top portion of bread to make a sandwich. Repeat with remaining sandwiches.

Remoulade Sauce:

- Place all ingredients into a blend but the mayonnaise and pulse together for a minute. Pour into bowl and add mayonnaise. Mix together. Chill in refrigerator until ready to serve.

## Nutrition Info

Calories: 511, Total Fat: 37g, Saturated Fat: 13g, Protein: 40g

# Fish Fillet Sandwiches

## Ingredients

- 4 frozen 97% fat-free baked breaded fish fillets or patties
- 1/3 cup fat-free mayonnaise or salad dressing
- 1 tablespoon pickle relish
- 2 whole wheat sandwich buns, split, toasted
- 2 (3/4-oz.) slices light American cheese

## Instructions

- Prepare fish fillets as directed on package.
- Meanwhile, in small bowl, combine mayonnaise and relish; mix well. Spread cut sides of buns with mayonnaise mixture. Place 2 fish fillets on bottom of each bun; top with cheese and cover with top of bun.

## Nutrition Info

Calories 370 Calories from Fat 80 Total Fat 9g Total Carbohydrate 51g Protein 20g

# Crispy Fish Sandwiches with Wasabi and Ginger

Prep/Cook Time: 15 - 45 mins, Servings: 4

## Ingredients

- 1/2 cup mayonnaise
- 1 medium lime, finely grated to Servings 1/2 tsp. zest and squeezed to Servings 4 tsp. juice
- 1-1/2 tsp. wasabi paste; more to taste
- Kosher salt and freshly ground black pepper
- 2 large eggs
- 2 Tbs. soy sauce
- 1 cup panko
- 4 4- to 5- oz. boneless, skinless hake, haddock, or cod fillets (preferably 1 to 1-1/2 inches thick)
- 1/2 cup plus 1 Tbs. vegetable oil
- 1 tsp. finely grated fresh ginger
- 3 cups thinly sliced iceberg lettuce (about 1/4 head)
- 4 hamburger buns, lightly toasted

## Instructions

- In a small bowl, combine the mayonnaise, lime zest, 1 tsp. of the lime juice, and the wasabi paste. Season to taste with salt, pepper, and more wasabi, if you like.
- In a wide, shallow bowl, lightly beat the eggs and 1 Tbs. of the soy sauce until combined. Put the panko in another wide shallow bowl.
- Pat the fish fillets dry and lightly season with salt. Working with one fillet at a time, dip it in the egg

78

mixture, letting any excess drip off, then coat with the panko, pressing the breadcrumbs onto the fish. Set each breaded fillet on a plate or tray as you finish it.

- In a 10-inch nonstick skillet, heat 1/2 cup of the oil over medium heat until shimmering hot. Fry the fish, flipping once, until well browned and just cooked through, 5 to 8 minutes total. Transfer to paper towels to drain and sprinkle each fillet with a pinch of salt.
- Meanwhile, in a large bowl, stir together the remaining 1 Tbs. lime juice, 1 Tbs. soy sauce, 1 Tbs. oil, the ginger, 1/4 tsp. salt, and 1/4 tsp. pepper. Add the lettuce and toss to coat.
- Spread the wasabi mayonnaise on both cut sides of the buns. Put one fish fillet on the bottom of each bun, and then top with the lettuce and the bun top.

*Nutrition Info*

Calories: 228 Fat: 11 Carbohydrates: 6 Protein: 23

# BEEF SANDWICHES

## Roast Beef Sandwiches with Caramelized Onions

*Prep/Cook Time 50 min, Servings 6*

### Ingredients

- 1 can (11 oz) Pillsbury™ refrigerated French bread
- 2 tablespoons butter or margarine
- 1 red onion, sliced, separated into rings
- 1 tablespoon packed brown sugar
- 1 tablespoon water
- 1/4 cup Dijon mustard
- 1 lb thinly sliced cooked roast beef (from deli)
- 10 slices (3/4 oz each) provolone cheese

### Instructions

- Heat oven to 350°F. Spray cookie sheet with cooking spray. Place loaf of dough, seam side down, on cookie sheet. With sharp knife, make 4 or 5 diagonal cuts (1/4 inch deep) in top of loaf.
- Bake 26 to 30 minutes or until loaf is golden brown. Cool completely, about 20 minutes.
- Meanwhile, in large skillet, melt butter over medium-high heat. Add onions and brown sugar. Cook 10 minutes, stirring occasionally, until onions are tender. Add water. Reduce heat to medium-low; cook 10 to 15

minutes, stirring occasionally, until onions are golden and glazed.

- Set oven control to broil. Cut loaf in half lengthwise. Spread mustard over cut sides of loaf. Top each half with roast beef, onions and cheese. Place sandwich halves on cookie sheet.
- Broil with tops about 3 inches from heat 2 to 3 minutes or until cheese is melted and light golden brown. Cut into slices to serve.

### Nutrition Info

Calories 406 Total Fat 17g Saturated Fat 10g Sodium 1229mg Total Carbohydrate 33g

# Slow Cooker Italian Beef for Sandwiches

Prep/Cook Time: 12 hrs 15 mins, Servings: 10

## Ingredient

- o 3 cups water
- o 1 teaspoon salt
- o 1 teaspoon ground black pepper
- o 1 teaspoon dried oregano
- o 1 teaspoon dried basil
- o 1 teaspoon onion salt
- o 1 teaspoon dried parsley
- o 1 teaspoon garlic powder
- o 1 bay leaf
- o 1 (.7 ounce) package dry Italian-style salad dressing mix
- o 1 (5 pound) rump roast

## Instructions

- Combine water with salt, ground black pepper, oregano, basil, onion salt, parsley, garlic powder, bay leaf, and salad dressing mix in a saucepan. Stir well, and bring to a boil.
- Place roast in slow cooker, and pour salad dressing mixture over the meat.
- Cover, and cook on Low for 10 to 12 hours, or on High for 4 to 5 hours. When done, remove bay leaf, and shred meat with a fork.

*Nutrition Info* : 318.2 calories; protein 39.4g 79% DV; carbohydrates 1.6g 1% DV; fat 15.8g 24% DV; cholesterol 100.4mg 34% DV; sodium 819.1mg

# Sweet & Spicy Roast Beef Sandwiches

Prep/Cook Time: 15 m, Servings: 4

## Ingredients

- 1 to 2 tablespoons prepared horseradish
- ⅓ cup mayonnaise
- 1 teaspoon Worcestershire sauce
- salt and freshly ground black pepper
- 4 crusty long steak rolls or hearty kaiser rolls
- 12 ounces sliced provolone cheese
- ¾ pound shaved or thinly sliced roast beef
- ½ cup bread and butter pickle chips
- 1 cup sliced roasted red pepper
- ½ teaspoon dried oregano

## Instructions

- Combine the horseradish, mayonnaise and Worcestershire sauce in a small bowl. (If you like things on the spicy side, add more horseradish; if you want to keep the spice level low, add less horseradish.) Season with freshly ground black pepper and set aside.
- Cut the rolls open, but not all the way through. Spread the horseradish mayonnaise on both sides of the bread. Add a couple slices of provolone cheese, laying them over both sides of the roll. Top with roast beef and nestle the pickles and roasted red peppers on the roast beef near the fold of the roll. Season with oregano, salt and freshly ground black pepper. Close the rolls and wrap with parchment paper to keep them closed.

- If you want to make these sandwiches ahead of time, rearrange how you build them as follows. First dry the pickles and red pepper strips with clean kitchen towel. Build the sandwiches by layering 2 slices of provolone cheese, laying them over both sides of the rolls. Spread some of the horseradish mayo on the cheese and then top with the roast beef. Place the dried roasted peppers and pickles on the roast beef near the fold of the roll. Season with oregano, salt and freshly ground black pepper. Close the sandwich making sure the roasted peppers and pickles are on the inside to ensure the bread does not become soggy. Wrap with parchment paper or aluminum foil.
- If you are not eating the sandwiches right away, store them in the refrigerator until you are ready to serve.
- When ready to serve, enjoy the sandwich cold with some potato chips or heat the sandwiches. You can heat them wrapped in foil on a BBQ grill for 5 to 6 minutes or unwrapped in your air fryer for 3 to 4 minutes – just enough for the cheese to melt and for the bread to get crusty. Let the hot sandwiches rest a few minutes before serving. Carefully unwrap and enjoy!

*Nutrition Info*

Calories: 378kcal, Fat: 8g, Saturated Fat: 5g, Cholesterol: 22mg, Sodium: 108mg, Potassium: 23mg

# Ultimate leftover beef sandwiches recipe

Prep/cook Time: 23 mins, Serves 2

## Ingredients

- o  4 slices leftover roast beef
- o  4 Tesco Finest mini San Marzano tomatoes, halved lengthways
- o  pinch dried oregano
- o  1 tbsp olive oil
- o  1 Tesco Finest ciabatta loaf
- o  1 garlic clove, halved lengthways
- o  4 tsp horseradish sauce
- o  2 handfuls rocket

## Instructions

- •  Preheat the oven to gas 6, 200°C, fan 180°C. Allow the beef slices to come to room temperature.
- •  Meanwhile, put the tomatoes in a small oven dish and top with a pinch of salt and oregano and 1/2 tsp of the oil. Put in the oven along with the ciabatta.
- •  Remove the bread after 8 minutes but leave the tomatoes to roast for a further 10 minutes. Meanwhile, heat a griddle pan over a medium heat.
- •  Cut the bread in half and then cut each half open. Brush the insides with remaining olive oil, then griddle until lightly charred. Rub the charred sides with the cut sides of the garlic cloves.
- •  Spread half the horseradish over one piece of the toasted ciabatta, top with a couple of slices of beef, season with

salt and pepper and then top with a handful of rocket and some roasted tomatoes. Sandwich with the other piece of toasted ciabatta and repeat to make the second sandwich. Serve immediately.

## Nutrition Info

Calories: 529kcal Fat 14g Saturates 3g Sugars 7g Salt 1.9g Carbohydrate 72.9g Protein 32.2g Fibre 5.8g

# Roast Beef Sandwiches

Prep/Cook Time: 1 hr 30 min, Servings: 6 main-course

## Ingredients

- 1 medium red onion, halved and thinly sliced
- 1 tablespoon, plus 2 teaspoons kosher salt, plus more to taste
- 6 tablespoons red wine vinegar
- 3/4 cup mayonnaise
- 3/4 cup sour cream
- 1/4 cup plus 2 tablespoons jarred grated horseradish (with liquid)
- 1/2 teaspoon grated lemon zest
- Freshly ground black pepper
- Hot sauce
- 6 Kaiser rolls
- 12 slices vine-ripened tomatoes
- 24 ounces freshly sliced rare roast beef
- 3 loosely packed cups watercress or arugula, or a combination of both

## Instructions

- In a small bowl, mix together the onion and 1 tablespoon of the salt. Set aside for 20 minutes. Rinse the onions with cold running water. Drain and squeeze to remove excess liquid. Combine the onions and the vinegar and marinate at least 30 minutes or up to 24 hours.
- In a small bowl, mix together the mayonnaise, sour cream, horseradish, zest, and 2 teaspoons salt. Season

generously with pepper and hot sauce to taste. Refrigerate the horseradish sauce for at least 30 minutes.

- Preheat the broiler. Slice the rolls in half lengthwise. Using your hands, shallowly scoop out the inside of each half. Transfer the rolls to a baking sheet and arrange scooped-side up. Toast the rolls under the broiler for about 1 minute. Slather the inside of the rolls with the horseradish sauce. On each of the roll bottoms, layer 2 tomato slices and season with salt and pepper to taste. Top the tomatoes with some of the roast beef overlapped into "ruffles" and season with salt and pepper. Top the meat with some of the onions and watercress and cover with the tops of the roll. Serve immediately.

## Nutrition Info

Calories: 306, Total Fat: 30.9g, Carbohydrates: 7.4g, Dietary Fiber: 1.6g, Protein: 44g

# GLUTEN-FREE SANDWICHES

## Gluten-free chicken salad sandwich

Prep/Cook Time: 15 mins, Servings: 4

### Ingredients

- 2 slices Coles Gluten Free Bread
- 2 tsp gluten-free whole-egg mayonnaise
- 1/2 cup shredded cooked chicken breast fillet
- 1/4 cup coarsely grated carrot
- 15g baby spinach leaves

### Instructions

- Spread 1 slice of bread with mayonnaise. Top with chicken, carrot and spinach. Top with remaining bread. Cut in half.

### Nutrition Info

Calories: 312, Total Fat: 18.2g, Carbohydrates: 3.8g, Fiber: 0.3g, Protein: 22.6g

# Ham, Egg & Cheese Gluten Free Sandwich

Prep/Cook Time 10 minutes, Servings 1

## Ingredients

- 1 egg scrambled
- 1 slice ham gluten free, smoked and thinly sliced
- 1 slice provolone cheese vegan or dairy free
- 2 slices gluten free bread Canyon Bakehouse Hawaiian Sweet Bread

## Instructions

- In a small pan on medium heat, cook your egg like an omelette only flipping it once until it's cooked all the way through.
- While the egg cooks, get out the rest of the ingredients.
- Optional: cut the bread, ham and cheese into flower or fun shapes.
- Transfer the cooked egg onto a cutting board and place the cheese on top of it. If you're cutting out shapes, do that first.
- Let it cool for 5 minutes.
- Stack your sandwich by placing a piece of bread on the bottom, then cheese, then egg, then ham, another layer of egg, cheese and the piece of bread on top.
- Enjoy!

Recipe Notes

If your child is too small to have a double layered sandwich, then only use one layer of egg, ham and cheese instead.

*Nutrition Info*

Calories 415 Calories from Fat 180, Fat 20g, Saturated Fat 7g, Cholesterol 212mg, Sodium 871mg, Potassium 179mg, Carbohydrates 31g, Fiber 1g, Sugar 4g, Protein 21g

Prep/Cooking time: 70 mins, Serves: 4 people

## Ingredients

For the bread
- 450g gluten free white bread flour plus extra for sprinkling
- 1 tsp salt
- 1 tbsp caster sugar
- 2 tsp fast action dried yeast
- 2 medium eggs
- 200ml semi-skimmed milk plus extra for glazing
- 150ml warm water
- 4 tbsp vegetable oil plus extra for oiling
- 1 tbsp white wine vinegar

For the fillings
- 2 medium eggs
- 1 tbsp mayonnaise
- ½ punnet salad cress
- 15g butter, at room temperature
- 100g smoked salmon
- 3tbsp cream cheese
- ½ lemon, to taste

## Instructions
- Place the flour, salt, sugar and yeast in the Kenwood Chef bowl fitted with the dough hook. Add the eggs, milk, water, vegetable oil and vinegar to the bowl. Mix on a low speed until all the ingredients are combined,

then scrape down any mixture from the sides of the bowl. Knead on a medium speed for 5 minutes. The dough will have a loose consistency.

- Brush a 1kg loaf tin with vegetable oil. Place the mixture in the prepared tin. Cover loosely with oiled cling film and set aside to rise for 1 hour or until doubled in size.
- Preheat the oven to 200C/gas mark 6.
- Brush the loaf with milk and sprinkle with a little flour. Bake for 25-30 minutes or until risen and golden. Transfer to a wire rack and set aside to cool completely.
- For the egg and cress filling, place the eggs in a small pan of cold water, bring to the boil and boil for 10 minutes. Drain and cool under cold running water. Peel the shells off, roughly chop the eggs and place in a bowl. Add the mayonnaise and cress and season to taste. Chill until ready to use.
- Once the bread is completely cold, trim off the ends and cut it into 12 slices. Spread half of the slices of bread with the butter. Spread the remaining slices with cream cheese.
- Divide the egg mixture between half the buttered slices of bread and top with the remaining buttered slices. Divide the smoked salmon between half the bread spread with cream cheese, season to taste with black pepper and a squeeze of lemon juice. Top with the remaining bread spread with cream cheese. Cut the filled sandwiches in half and serve straight away.

*Nutrition Info*

Calories 345, Calories from Fat 90, Fat 10g, Saturated Fat 1g, Carbohydrates 10g, Fiber 4g, Protein 26g

# Gluten-Free Finger Sandwiches

A one-bite appetizer that will accommodate guests with dietary restrictions.

Prep/Cook Time 10 min, Serves 6

## Ingredients

- 6 slices Schär Gluten-Free Artisan Baker Multigrain Bread
- 1/4 cup cucumbers, peeled and sliced into quarter moons
- 2 oz smoked salmon, cut into 1-inch pieces
- 1/4 cup peanut butter
- 1/4 cup jelly
- 1 ounce mozzarella, cut into 1-inch pieces
- 1/2 tomato, cut into 1-inch pieces
- 36 toothpicks

## Instructions

- Slices crusts off of bread and cut each bread slice into six squares.
- Divide bread squares into three groups.
- In the first group of squares, spread each slice of bread with cream cheese.
- Place salmon and cucumber in between two slices and secure with toothpick.
- Repeat for remaining five sandwiches.

- For the next group of squares, speed one half of each slice with peanut butter and the other with jelly.
- Secure each sandwich with a toothpick.
- For the last group of square, place mozzarella and tomato between two slices and secure with a toothpick.

## Nutrition Info

Calories 157, Calories from Fat 117, Fat 13g, Protein 3.9g

# Gluten-free Triple Meat Sandwich

## Ingredients

For each sandwich:

- 2 slices Canyon Bakehouse gluten-free Heritage Loaf Honey White or Whole Grain bread
- 3 thin slices smoked turkey
- 2 slices roast beef
- 2 slices smoked ham
- 2 slices colby jack cheese (or other favorite cheese)
- 1 slice sharp cheddar cheese
- 2-3 slices tomato
- 1-2 sections of green leaf lettuce
- mustard and mayo as desired

## Instructions

- Layer all ingredients the way you like them between two slices of Heritage Loaf bread.
- Enjoy!

## Nutrition Info

Calories: 354kcal, Carbohydrates: 11g, Protein: 53g, Fat: 10g, Saturated Fat: 6g, Cholesterol: 138mg, Sodium: 657mg

## Grilled Cheese-Burger Sandwiches

Servings: 4 people

*Ingredients*

- o sliced bread
- o butter
- o cheese, sliced
- o leftover meatloaf, sliced and brought to room temperature

*Instructions*

- Round up your ingredients. Heat your pan on the stove top to low-medium heat. *Optional: Preheat your oven to 400F.
- Butter one side of your bread slices. Put buttered side down on your pan. Add a slice of cheese, meatloaf, another slice of cheese and another buttered slice of bread to finish the sandwich.
- Cook until the bread is browned and cheese is slightly melted. *Optional: You can finish off the sandwiches in a preheated oven for about 5 minutes to assure the sandwich has been heated through. Depending on the thickness of your sandwich this may not be needed.

*Nutrition Info*

Calories 367 Calories from Fat 171, Fat 19g, Saturated Fat 7g, Carbohydrates 7g, Fiber 1g, Sugar 1g, Protein 34g

# Hamburger Recipe

## *Ingredients*

Hamburger Pattie

- 800g - 1kg, 1.6 - 2 lb ground beef (mince), 20% + fat (Note 1)
- Salt and pepper
- 3 onions, peeled and sliced into rings
- 2 tbsp oil
- 4 - 8 slices cheese of choice, I use Swiss (optional)

Hamburger

- 4 soft hamburger buns, lightly toasted
- Lettuce, tomato slices
- Ketchup, mustard, relish, sliced pickles

## *Instructions*

- Separate beef into 4 equal portions. Use hands to lightly form into patties the size of your buns (mine are about 10 cm, 4") - don't press hard, light fingers = soft juicy patties.
- Season generously with salt and pepper on both sides. Make a dent on one side (stop burger from become dome shape and shrinking when cooking).

- Heat 1 tbsp oil in a heavy based skillet or BBQ over high heat. Add onion and cook until wilted and caramelised. Season with salt and pepper, then remove.
- Heat 1 tbsp oil until smoking. Add patties and cook for 2 minutes until deep golden with a great crust. Do not press! Flip carefully, cook for 1 minute then top with cheese (if using). Cover with lid and cook for further 1 minute until cheese is melted.
- Meanwhile, toast the cut side of the buns lightly.
- To serve: Spread base of buns with sauce, condiment of choice. Top with lettuce then tomato, then hamburger patty. Pile over onions, sliced pickles, then more sauce/condiments. Top with lid of bun. Serve immediately.

*Nutrition Info*

Calories 400, Fat 20g, Protein 19.4g

# Souperburger Sandwiches

Prep/Cook Time 25 minutes, serves 6 people

## Ingredients

- o 1 pound ground beef
- o 1 medium onion, chopped (about 1/2 cup)
- o 1 can (10 3/4 ounces) Campbell's® Condensed Tomato Soup
- o 1 tablespoon yellow mustard
- o 1/8 teaspoon black pepper
- o 6 Pepperidge Farm® Sesame Topped Hamburger Buns

## Instructions

- Cook the beef and onion in a 10-inch skillet over medium-high heat until the beef is well browned, stirring often. Pour off any fat.
- Stir the soup, mustard and black pepper in the skillet and cook until the mixture is hot and bubbling. Divide the beef mixture among the rolls.

## Nutrition Info

Calories: 430, Fat: 199, Carbohydrates: 4g, Fiber: 1g, Protein: 54g

# Bacon Double Cheeseburger Grilled Cheese

Prep/Cook Time:25 minutes, Servings: 1

## Ingredients

- 2 strips bacon, cut into 1 inch pieces
- 1/2 small onion, diced
- 1 clove garlic, chopped
- 1/4 pound ground beef
- 1 tablespoon ketchup
- 1 teaspoon mustard
- 1/2 teaspoon worcestershire sauce
- salt and pepper or steak seasoning to taste
- 2 slices bread
- 1 tablespoon butter
- 1/4 cup cheddar, shredded
- 1/4 cup mozzarella, shredded
- 1/4 cup lettuce, shredded
- 1/4 cup tomatoes, diced
- 1 tablespoon pickle, diced

## Instructions

- Cook the bacon in a pan over medium heat, set aside on paper towels to drain reserving 1 teaspoon of grease in the pan and the rest elsewhere.
- Add the onion and saute until tender, about 5-7 minutes.
- Add the garlic and saute until fragrant, about a minute.
- Add the ground beef and cook draining any grease when done.

- Mix in the ketchup, mustard, worcestershire sauce, salt and pepper, simmer to reduce, remove from heat and set aside.
- Heat a clean pan over medium heat.
- Butter the outside side of each slice of bread, place one slice in a pan buttered side down, sprinkle on half of the cheese, then top with the the bacon, beef, lettuce, tomato and pickle followed by the remaining cheese and slice of bread, buttered side up.
- Cook until golden brown on both sides and the cheese is melted, about 2-4 minutes per side.

### *Nutrition Info*

Calories: 321, Fat: 16g, Saturated Fat: 9g, Cholesterol: 308mg, Carbohydrates: 23g, Fiber: 2g, Sugar: 6g, Protein: 33g

# Toasty Grilled Beef and Cheese

## Ingredients:

- 1 pound Certified Angus Beef ® ground chuck
- 1 cup chopped mushrooms
- 1/2 small onion, finely chopped
- 1 clove garlic, minced
- 4 teaspoons butter
- 8 slices white bread
- 8 slices Swiss cheese

## Instructions:

- Brown ground chuck in medium frying pan with mushrooms, onion and garlic. Drain excess fat; remove beef mixture from pan and wipe pan clean.
- Melt 1 teaspoon butter over medium-high heat in the same pan. Brown two slices of bread. Flip bread over and top each with one slice Swiss cheese. Top one slice of bread with 1/3 to 1/2 cup hamburger mixture. Place second slice of toasted bread on top and flip sandwich over one more time to melt cheese.
- Keep prepared Toasty Grilled Beef and Cheese sandwiches warm in oven while cooking the others.

## Nutrition Info

Calories: 324kcal, Carbohydrates: 19g, Protein: 50g, Fat: 16g

## Grilled French Bread Dessert Sandwiches

Prep/Cook Time: 23 min, Servings: 2 to 4

### Ingredients

- Nonstick, nonflammable cooking spray
- 1/2 pint strawberries
- 3 to 4 tablespoons sugar
- 1/4 cup warm water
- 8 (1-inch thick) French bread slices
- 4 tablespoons marshmallow creme, divided
- 4 tablespoons chocolate hazelnut flavored spread, divided
- 2 bananas, sliced
- 1/4 cup (1/2 stick) butter, melted

### Instructions

- Spray the grill rack with nonstick, nonflammable cooking spray. Preheat the grill to medium heat.
- In a small bowl, add the strawberries, sugar, and warm water. Set aside. The sugar will dissolve and create a syrup.
- Spread 1 side of half of the bread slices with about 1 tablespoon marshmallow creme. Spread 1 side of the remaining bread slices with about 1 tablespoon chocolate hazelnut spread. Place sliced bananas on top. Top each marshmallow creme bread slice with a

chocolate hazelnut bread slice to make a sandwich. Brush the outsides of the sandwiches evenly with the melted butter.

- Grill the sandwiches until the bread is toasted and the marshmallow creme has melted, about 2 minutes per side. Drizzle with the strawberries and their syrup on top and serve immediately.

# Ice Cream Sandwich Cake

## Ingredient

- 24 eaches vanilla ice cream sandwiches, unwrapped
- 2 (8 ounce) containers whipped topping (such as Cool Whip®), thawed
- 1 (12 ounce) jar hot fudge ice cream topping, warmed
- 1 (12 ounce) jar caramel ice cream topping
- ¼ cup chopped pecans, or to taste

## Instructions

- Arrange a layer of ice cream sandwiches in the bottom of a 9x13-inch dish; top with a layer of whipped topping, hot fudge topping, and caramel topping. Repeat layering with remaining ice cream sandwiches, whipped topping, hot fudge topping, and caramel topping, ending with a top layer of whipped topping. Sprinkle with pecans. Cover dish with aluminum foil and freeze until set, at least 30 minutes.

## Nutrition Info

576.1 calories; protein 6.5g 13% DV; carbohydrates 85.4g 28% DV; fat 24.8g 38% DV; cholesterol 39.8mg

# Vanilla Dessert Sandwiches

Prep/Cook Time: 70 mins, Servings: 24

## Ingredient

- o 3 cups unbleached all-purpose flour
- o 2 teaspoons cream of tartar
- o 1 teaspoon baking soda
- o ½ teaspoon salt
- o 1 cup unsalted butter, softened
- o 1 ½ cups granulated sugar
- o 2 tablespoons milk
- o 1 tablespoon vanilla extract
- o 1 teaspoon pure ground vanilla beans* or 2 tsp. vanilla extract
- o Vanilla sugar (recipe below)
- o 1 recipe Vanilla Cream Cheese Frosting

## Instructions

- In medium bowl whisk together flour, cream of tartar, baking soda, and salt. Set aside.
- In large bowl beat butter with an electric mixer on medium speed for 30 seconds. Add granulated sugar and beat until smooth and creamy. Beat in milk, vanilla, and ground vanilla. Beat in as much of the flour mixture as you can with the mixer. Stir in remaining flour mixture by hand. Dough will be soft.
- Divide dough in half. Cover and chill dough about 30 minutes or until easy to handle. On lightly floured surface, roll half the dough at a time until 1/8 inch thick.

- Preheat oven to 350 degrees F. Using a 3-inch round cookie cutter, cut out circles from dough. Using a 1-inch round cookie cutter, cut out circles from the centers of half the dough circles. Place dough circles on parchment paper-lined cookie sheets. Reroll scraps, including the 1-inch dough rounds, and cut out additional dough circles as directed. Repeat with remaining dough half.
- Sprinkle the dough circles that have the centers cut out with vanilla sugar. Bake cookies for 10 to 12 minutes or until golden brown. Let cookies cool on cookie sheets for 1 minute. Transfer cookies to wire racks to cool completely.
- Spread bottoms of the solid cookies with about 1-1/2 teaspoons of the Vanilla Cream Cheese Frosting. Top each with one of the cookies with the center hole, sugar side up. Refrigerate filled cookies to store. Makes 24 sandwich cookies.

*Nutrition Info*

223 calories; total fat 10g; saturated fat 6g; polyunsaturated fatg; monounsaturated fat 3g; cholesterol 28mg; sodium 126mg; potassium 74mg; carbohydrates 31g; fiberg; sugar 18g; protein 2g

# Chocolate Panini

*Prep/Cook Time 8 Mins, Servings 10 sandwiches*

## Ingredients

- 1 (8-ounce) loaf ciabatta bread 2 to 3 tablespoons olive oil 1 (4-ounce) bittersweet chocolate baking bar, coarsely chopped (we tested with Ghirardelli)

## Instructions

- Preheat panini press according to manufacturer's instructions.
- Slice bread into 10 (1") pieces; slice each piece in half. Brush crust sides of each piece of bread with olive oil. Turn bottoms of bread, oiled side down. Place chocolate evenly on bottom pieces of bread; cover with tops of bread, oiled side up.
- Place 5 sandwiches in panini press; cook 1 minute or just until chocolate begins to melt and bread is toasted. Repeat procedure with remaining sandwiches. Serve hot.

# Grilled Chocolate-Raspberry

Prep Time 5 Mins, Grill Time 4 Mins
Stand Time 1 Min, 4 servings

## Ingredients

- 1/4 cup seedless raspberry preserves
- 8 (1/4-inch) slices Portuguese, Italian, or round sourdough bread
- 12 (.53-ounce) packages truffle-filled dark chocolate squares or 2 (1.55-ounce) milk chocolate bars
- 8 teaspoons butter Coarse sea salt (optional)

## Instructions

- Preheat grill to medium heat (300°). Spread raspberry preserves on 1 side of bread slices. Place 2 chocolate squares or half milk chocolate bar in center of 4 slices. Top with remaining bread slices. Spread about 2 teaspoons butter on outsides of each sandwich.
- Grill sandwiches 2 minutes; carefully turn, and grill 2 more minutes or until bread is toasted and chocolate is soft. Sprinkle with sea salt, if desired. Let sandwiches stand 1 to 2 minutes, and cut in half.

## Nutrition Info

Calories Per Serving: 277, Total Fat 17.9g, Protein 20.2g

## Easy Ham and Cheese Appetizer Sandwiches

Prep/Cook Time: 30 mins, Servings: 12

### Ingredient

- o 1 cup butter, softened
- o 3 tablespoons poppy seeds
- o 1 onion, grated
- o 1 tablespoon Worcestershire sauce
- o 2 tablespoons prepared Dijon-style mustard
- o 2 (12 ounce) packages white party rolls
- o ½ pound chopped cooked ham
- o 5 ounces shredded Swiss cheese

### Instructions

- Preheat oven to 350 degrees F (175 degrees C).
- In a medium bowl, mix together butter, poppy seeds, onion, Worcestershire sauce and prepared Dijon-style mustard.
- Slice rolls in half horizontally and set aside tops. Spread bottoms with the butter mixture. Top with ham and Swiss cheese. Replace tops.
- Arrange rolls in a single layer in a medium baking dish. Bake in the preheated oven 10 to 12 minutes, until rolls are lightly browned and cheese is melted.

*Nutrition Info :* 416 calories; protein 12.1g; carbohydrates 31.4g; fat 27.2g; cholesterol 62.7mg

# Cucumber and Ham Snack Sandwiches

Prep/Cook Time 10 minutes, Servings 2

## Ingredient

- o  8 cucumber slices
- o  2 deli ham slices
- o  4 small Pepper Jack cheese slices (or cheese of your choice)
- o  toothpicks for serving

## Instructions

- Slice the cucumber.
- Cut each piece of ham in half, fold, and lay each piece on top of a cucumber slice.
- Slice the cheese and top each piece of ham.
- Add the remaining cucumber slices to the top of the sandwiches and secure with a toothpick. Serve!

## Nutrition Info

Calories: 277kcal, Carbohydrates: 24g, Protein: 22g, Fat: 10g, Saturated Fat: 2g, Cholesterol: 107mg, Sodium: 621mg

Prep/Cook Time: 15 minutes, Servings: 7

## Ingredients

- o  6 Townhouse Crackers
- o  2 slices oven roasted turkey breast, cut into small pieces
- o  2 slices provolone cheese, quartered (or cut into fun shapes with cookie cutters)
- o  4 Club Crackers
- o  1 slice mozzarella cheese, quartered (or cut into fun shapes with cookie cutters)
- o  4 slices turkey pepperoni
- o  4 Carr's Crackers
- o  1 slice Muenster cheese, quartered (or cut into fun shapes with cookie cutters)
- o  1 slice sharp cheddar cheese, quartered (or cut into fun shapes with cookie cutters)
- o  1-2 slices honey ham, cut into small pieces

## Instructions

- • Choose your cracker sandwich combination.
- • Layer your meats and cheeses on top of your crackers of choice.
- • Top with another cracker.
- • Serve immediately or pack in food storage containers to bring as snack kits on-the-go.

- • Make-Your-Own Option

- Pack a bento box lunchbox or a food storage container with several different crackers and toppings.
- Let people mix and match their cracker sandwiches when it's time to eat.

Notes

- Possibilities are endless. Mix and match your crackers, deli meats and cheeses to your heart's content. Add charcuterie, too, if your people dig that.
- Bring an ice pack and/or cooler to keep your ingredients cool when you're on the road.
- Keep the ingredients separate when you're keeping them cool. Keep the crackers at room temperature, out of the cooler, and build the sandwiches when it's time to eat.

*Nutrition Info*

Calories: 237 Total Fat: 12g Saturated Fat: 5g Unsaturated Fat: 6g Cholesterol: 38mg Sodium: 370mg Carbohydrates: 17g Fiber: 1g Sugar: 6g Protein: 15g

# Mini Sandwiches

Prep/Cook Time 15 minutes, Servings: 24 Pieces

## *Ingredients*

- o 4 tablespoons Cream Cheese, softened
- o 4 teaspoons Mustard
- o 6 Slices of Bread,
- o 6 Cheddar Cheese
- o 8 Slices of Deli Ham
- o Baby Lettuce Leaves

## *Instructions*

- In a bowl, mix cream cheese and mustard until smooth.
- Place 3 slices of bread on your worktop. Spread each with a thin layer of the cream cheese mixture (you should use about ½ of it).
- Now, take 2 slices of cheddar and place these on top of one slice. Add 1 or 2 slices of ham (see note 4) and top this with lettuce. Cover with second slice of bread and top this again with cheese (I only use 1 slice here), ham, lettuce and last slice of bread (spread side facing down). Press down slightly. Repeat the same with other 3 slices.
- Cut each sandwich in half. Stick 6 toothpicks into each half and cut around them. You will get 6 mini sandwiches out of 1 half = 12 mini sandwiches out of 1 sandwich. Sticking the toothpicks in before cutting keeps the fillings from moving and makes it easier to cut the tiny sandwiches.
- Transfer them onto a serving tray and enjoy!

*Nutrition Info :* Calories: 64 Total Fat: 4g Saturated Fat: 2g Unsaturated Fat: 1g Cholesterol: 12mg Sodium: 180mg Carbohydrates: 4g Sugar: 1g Protein: 4g

# Honey Butter Sandwich Recipe

Prep/Cook Time 10 mins, Serves: 2 sandwich

## Ingredients

- Bread Slices - 4
- Butter - 2 tblsp
- Honey - 2 tblsp
- Salt a pinch

## Instructions

- Take butter, honey and salt in a bowl and mix well.
- Take bread slices, apply butter on both sides.
- Cut it into pieces.
- Serve.

## Nutrition Info

Calories: 389kcal, Carbohydrates: 11g, Protein: 30g, Fat: 24g

# CONCLUSION

Building a better breakfast starts with the right kitchen tools. Tame busy mornings by equipping your kitchen with the best coffee maker, a convenient breakfast sandwich maker or a mess-free a waffle maker. Ban boring breakfasts and avoid the drive-through lines (and cost!) by using our espresso makers, personal oatmeal makers and toaster ovens. From lattes to smoothies, breakfast sandwiches to crunchy toast, our collection of essential breakfast small kitchen appliances will help you make the first meal of the day the best meal of the day.

Made in the USA
Coppell, TX
13 December 2020